An Oriental Marriage Tech - System

Dr. Shubha Chandra Mishra, Ph.D

GenNext Publication

Published by

GenNext Publication
5, Ansari Road
Daryaganj, New Delhi-110002
Phone: 011-47034999, 9811692060
E-mail: gennextpublication@hotmail.com

Distribution Network
gyanbooks.com
India, USA, Canada, UK, Australia, France

ISBN: 978-93-5663-289-9 (PB)
First Published, 2025
Printed at: Gyan Press, Delhi.

AN ORIENTAL MARRIAGE TECH - SYSTEM

Author: Dr. Shubha Chandra Mishra

An Oriental Marriage Tech - System

Contents

The profile

Name – Dr. Shubha Chandra Mishra
Father's Name –
Vidyavācaspati Late Babu Mishra

Postal Address –
Dr. (prof) Shubha Chandra Mishra
Ward No. 10
P.O. Jhanjharpur Bazar.
Dist. Madhubani (Bihar)-847404
Designation - Principal

M – 9939984914 / 7667921138
Email – drscmishra6@gmail.com

1. Academic qualification – M.A. Acharya. Ph.d.
2. Professional Qualificatioin –
    - a. U.G.C Sponsored R.C. Programme — Kurukshetra University Kurukshetra (Harayana) — Qualified- 1991 Qualified- 1991
    - b. Do (Auditions performance) — Lucknow university Lucknow (U.P) — do - 1991
    - c. do — University of Calicut Kerala) — selected 1992
    - d. do — Poona university, Pune (M.S) — Qualified 1995
    - e. Professional Development Programme (Officers) — University of Hyderabad, Hyderabad (A.P.) — 2009
3. Seminar/Workshop/Webinar
    - a. Bharvi's principle of life (Dais lecture) — -A partial fulfilment of R.C. programme -Poona University Pune (M.S.) — 1995
    - b. National ability in Chhatrapati charitam (Dais lecture) — Do — 1995
    - c. Workshop on Manuscriptology & Palaeograpy (3 weeks) by Indra Gandhi National Centre for the Arts, New Delhi — In collaboration with Poona University Pune (M.S) — 1995
    - d. Research Methodology in Indology — Mithila Institute of P.G. studies & research in Skt. Learning, Kabaraght (Darbhanga) Bihar — 2004

e.	National Seminar sponsored by U. G. C on post-Independence Skt. works on Indian Democracy	B.B.A. Bihar university Muzaffarpur (Bihar)	2007
f.	Learned speech on the great use of social service	Spl. Camp at Dr. J.M.S. College, pastan Navtoli (Madhuban) Bihar	2014
g.	Learned speech on Swami Vivekanand Jayanti & National Youth Day	Kalptaru Cultural Evolutional Trust, Ghaziabad (U.P)	2020

4. Project work/Research project

a.	Skt. teaching method	A partial fulfilment of the R.C. programe, Lucknow university, Lucknow (U.P)	
b.	An oriental approach to human globe	Indian institute of Advanced Study Rashtrapati Niwas, Shimala (H.P) The project appreciated and fellowship award constrained to limitation-	1997
c.	Minor U.G.C. research project-Supervisor	On Distingguished women in Krishna literature in Mithila Region.- a perception by Dr. Ravindra Nath Jha	2013-14

Book/Article published/underwork

5. Article published/underwork

a.	Chhatrapati charitam parichayah	Vishwamaniṣa Bulletin under K.S. D.S.U Darbanga (Bihar)	1981
b.	suddhādwet Ke pravartaka Acharya Ballava ka pustivāda	Mathureshwar jee Felicitation volume Raipur (M.P)	1994
c.	Common culture of Mithila & environment	Mithila institute of Skt. P.G. studies & Research, Darbhanga (Bihar)	2006
d.	Kalsarpayoga Mimānsā	Do (Śastrartha technical	2008
f.	Vidyāvācaspati pt. Baba Mishra- A commemoration	Esteemed Journal 'Sāstrārtha' M.I . skt. studies & research Darbhanga(Bihar)	2012
g.	Wine-shun in oriental opinion	Pratibimaba (Hly Journal) M.R.P.L. Manglore (Karnatak)	2015
h.	Awareness compaign for wine-shun	Ṣuggested to Govt. of Bihar	2017

i.	An Oriental Mission for Global Vision	-genNext (Gyan Books) publications New Delhi	2021
j.	An Oriental Infer-System on AL-I & Smart Justice	-genNext (Gyan Books) publications New Delhi	2024

6. Extra-curricular Activities

a.	Chief guest at Education & Cultural Conference on Yuva Avam Loktantra	Under the auspices of Nehru Yuva Kendra, Jhanjharpur (Madhubani)Bihar	1981
b.	Programme officer	Dr. J.M.S College pastan Navtoli (Madhubani)	1994-96
c.	As a Spl. Guest to deliver learned speech on Rastrapitā Gandhi & Village panchayāt	Inaugurated by Hon'ble M.P. (R.S.) M.L. Mandal at P. Raj. Ganauli Andharathadhi Madhubani (Bihar)	2004
d.	Nodal officer (C. unit) (NMEICT)	National Mission for Education through Information & Communication Technology, MHRD, New Delhi.	2010-11
e.	Analyst (Swot & Rusa)-Institutional Development planning & 20-point theme for NEP, MHRD, New Delhi	To the State of Bihar (Educational Deptt.) Patna & MHRD, New Delhi	2014-15
f.	Ex-officio member in University Selection Board. K.S.D.S. University, Darbhanga	Constituted to Dr. R.K.T.J college. Ekahari (Ladania) Madbhubani	2014-16
g.	Ex-officio member (Counselling Committee)	NAAC Peer Team, Banglore for K.S.D.S.U (Darbhanga), Bihar	2016

The Prelude

Human beings are kindred species and their affinity in marriage is the holy union and the declaration of deep appreciation and commitment. It is the legacy from God-made before friends and family near altar (focal point) around the sanctum. Holy matrimony is devoted to human love, erotic flavor and procreation for noble end. The couple receives solemn blessings from deities for pomp & pleasure.

In Hindu Law there are 08 forms of marriage namely

(1) Brahma vivāh

(2) Deva (deity) vivāh

(3) Arsha vivāh- a from of marriage of Rishi dynasty in which the father of the bride used to receive one or two cows (resources for nourishment) from the groom side.

(4) Prājāpatya vivāh– relating to prājāpati in which the father gives his daughter to the groom without receiving any gift or dowry from the groom side in order to live together faithfully. Since Hindu scriptures suggest for the groom (receiver of gift or dowry) being slāve to her family and their issues be called Dās.

(5) Asur vivāh – evil spirits

(6) Gandharva vivāh – A class of demi god professed celestial musicians and said to have nice voice to the bride.

(7) Rākshasa vivāh – demoniacal nature in which a maid is seized forcibly and carried away on defeat or demolition of her relatives in battle.

(8) Paishāch vivāh – the lowest form of marriage in which a lover commits rape upon the maid against her wishes in slumber or intoxication.

Here mind that donation/dowry against bride means that of her clan to his clan for progeny, prestige and protection as life-partners. She wields will power for adroitness and process to handle and propel conjugal life in all situations.

Now the people live on wheels hovering about the globe and thereby tasting across varied culture during their life span. They are ready to imbibe the essence of those strange culture as well. They adopt some sorts of varied rituals in their ceremonial events.

Here I am concerned with marriage rituals to sanctify its significance since vedic period down to the current one.

In such vein I would like to narrate categorically the following mixed events –

(a) Ring ceremony – wedding ring denotes virtues, delight, festive Jubilee, commitment, resolution positive, fidelity and dignity. Further it represents the consummate concurrence of the couple towards steady wed-lock. The brand of novel sacrament ionised with its ring circle is imposed for social, ritual and legal performance. Its circular shape stands for its perennial passion sans initial to ending point.

(b) Feast ceremony – The bride-members and associates go to the groom's house to celebrate investiture-ceremony with feast in course of soliciting the groom. Here the bride-members offer apparel, ornament and cosmetics in honour of treating him (groom) as lord Vishnu.

(c) Turmerico – Henna tattoo ceremony – it is a pre-wedding ritual. It is assumed to cleanse the negative energy of the couple and protect them against evil spirits. Its bright yellow colour is considered auspicious and symbolizes a happy start-up to a new life togetherly.

Thanks to the millennia of our oriento-racial or multiculti flavor to celebrate in majestic manners. Now the significance of applying turmeric paste to the bride and the groom is to discharge skin-flaws. Because it is antimicrobial and anti inflammatory. It has anti-oxidant called curcumin to soothe mental commotion. So besides its charming property, it is believed to reduce apprehension of conjugal life to be intered into the next span of career.

Further its yellow colour stands for happiness, humour, optimism, wisdom, divine essence and glory between the couple. It wards off anti-energy or evil spirits for a new life in honey moon.

(d) Henna ceremony – In oriental culture, henna paste is applied to lessen anxiety, burning to muscular region. It is supposed to enhance health and hygience in sound fondness and passion between the couple. It represents the union of matrimony as a token of gaiety and mutual move for their marriage journey or voyage. It has medicinal property to reduce stress and excitement entangled with neural alignment rolling between the bride and the goom.

It guards the couple against viral ailments and secures blood circulation for conjugal charms.

Further it enhances the pomp & honour with affection and analogy within the wedding serials. Its scent is associated with ornamental lustre.

(e) Socio-marriage registration – The bio-conception of erotic fondness rests on opposite clans, kins and species. So it is essential to reach out and match contra-bio pairs declared on the palm leaves by the social Registrar. Though the guy-folk happen to be ready to live with cognate mates out of imbalance of bodily humours as exceptional cases. But the nobility of thoughts bans such evil practice. It is a mood disorder that is sub-type of major depressive disorder (MDD) melancholia. It relates to erotic melancholia suffering from excessive guilt, feeling of hopelessness and thoughts of suicide. Anyhow social approval is needed for flawless wedlock.

(f) Plant-based pre-marriage ceremony – In order to avert evil effects of Mangal dosha (planetary Mars fault) the bride has to under-go some ritual as anti-planetary device. Such ritual wards off mishappenings or catastrophe as in horoscope.

When the Mars resides in the 1st, 4th, 7th, 8th or 12th house in one's horoscope one has to celebrate plant-based pre-marriage ceremony. Here mind that when Mars resides in Gemini, virgo, Libra or Taurus zodiacal sign, no mishappening is effective in conjugal life. Otherwise Mars anti-effect would cause marriage break-through, serious blood related eruption, frailty, heinous crimes, and bitterness in conjugal life or any family foes.

In other way the parents are suggested to search boys and girls having Mars fault both to have cut-across each other's anti-effects.

As confirmation to avert mishappenigns due to Mars blemish we are adviced to get married to mango (Mangifera Indica) tree linked with goddess Laxmi and Ambika + butter – cup tree (Mahuca Longifolia) with yellow fibre locking and vermition applied.

(g) Cow-gifting – According to the Atharvaveda (Life-hygienic science), cow is the source of all holy life serving like motherhood and mother-earth. It damns all slaughter of men, cattle and prays to god Agni to penalize those who slay.

All vedic rituals are done with cow butter (ghee) for oblation and invocation befitting all creature. Cow is goddess in paradise being capable of granting all ethical/moral wishes and desires as kāmdhenu associated with lord Indra. She serves as angelic and natural agent to be cared for about 33 categories of deity dwelling within herself.

Cow is connected with lord Krishna being cow-herd while fluting.

Cow is also associated with lord shiva in the form of Nandi-bull.

So back to the vedic period the veneration of cow is traced out as motherly love, wealth (milk hygiene), nourishment (ghee-butter). Cow has healing properties being productive of milk, curd, butter, urine and dung.

Thus reverential adoption of cow is justified in all rituals and rites.

(h) Sacrificial oblation to the Fire. Here the Fire represents tie between angelical and mortal globe. It is life giver (energy) and life-taker (ashes). Heat and energy is the realm of agni which stands for the transformation of the gross into the subtle. Agni wards off nescience. Agni was born when the sun became visible. The existence of Fire-god stands for divine light and energy that transforms our mindset for cordial sanctity. There is no fire without energy-fire within us. It has life force and digestive power to boost up our health, hygiene and humours. Further Fire-god stands for fortitude and firmness of fidelity to live in joint venture of conjugal life.

He is believed to be the token of divine presence, glory, justice, sanctity and redemption. He is life tonic or progenitor and lyncher.

Although fire may indicate the sun, the cosmets, sacrificial funeral pyre and digestive trait.

The prime-god presiding over Creation and the Fire god being the father-son in mystical events united into one Self as the undying identity of the universe in the form of prapapati, varuna, Indra, Rudra, Sāvitree, vāyu, gāyatri and the like manifestations. Since the Fire god is believed to have stemmed from the mouth of the Cosmic lord (prajāpati) being Vishnu after being born from the Brahma.

He (Fire god) was married to swāhā having shuchi out of 03 sons and one sister called medhā.

Therefore the presence of the Fire-god is justified for their welfare.

(i) Saptapadee (Septa-step around) the Fire-god) – Here 07 – digit signifies divine love namely – affection (2nd name of ghee-cleared butter), sympathy, service, feeling, kindness, self-interest or feeling of meum. Here ghee oblation to the fire makes the deity delightful with these divine love.

The sun remits 07 colours representing 07 horses in his chariot as follows-

Prajāpati	–	God
Indra	–	the self
Agni	–	Splendour
Soma	–	Peace
Bhooh	–	The physique
Bhuvah	–	The Mind
Swah	–	Conscience (the seat of thought & feeling)

07 round-pics made of powdered rice (called pithar) are depicted to wish for god's grace personifying the bride. In primitive ages the aripan (pithar rangoli) refers to smear the earth with cowdung and clay for fertile and fruitful land to the extent of purification (antiworn drive).

As per procedure, the couple's 07 – step is revered to recognize her grandeur. The 7th generation between 02 – term that refers to the parents intermingling of 02-family in their course or succession in the scale of genealogical descending.

Because the generation is considered family-oriented values, diversity, self expression, social responsibility, environment and behavior. You bring up children which impact not only him or her but 04 generations that follow.

(j) Bride gifting – the bride is bestowed to the groom as possession. Here is the publicized giving away in charity which confers courtesy and cordiality shown in wide feeling and acquiescence by the groom. Both partners have theological virtues by which the both pray the Almighty jointly for their own sake. Both should have charitable hearts to love for the whole of creation smoothly on non-profit footing. Both should be conscious of their offerings and understanding of their obligations.

But it should be borne in mind that such giving away or bestowing the bride has some unusual meaning in the sense that her performance or service is reversible to her paternal mates if the awkward situation commands. So it is against the usual nature of charity or donation in toto regarding goods or stuff.

To be more clear the bride donor does not give away his whole sovereignty to the groom rather beslows her to treat as his (groom) better-part in usual understanding. It is unlike cow donation in toto having no cause for reversion. It may be just like giving garments to the washerman.

(k) Acquarius pitcher – pre-marriage ceremony to avert mishappenings a girl or a bride is suggested to get married to the pitcher crowned with gold locket or ring at papal tree (Ficus religiosa) root in the guise of lord Vishnu. Here the worship goes through exhaustive technicalities ending girl bath with sacred water-resources.

(l) Groom observation – The groom has to face cross observation, as it were, to assess for repairers (thaka) of marriage conflicts on rumours or reminding to delete anti-communications. At the same time the groom is suggested to connive at pretender or Pecksniffian showing crane-cunning bird (vaka)

Banana tender leaves to assess and affirm heart-throbbing compression due to be entered into conjugal life. Special grass string (shami), betel leaves and lit-up lamp in tortoise skull is shown to ward off evil spirits through mental smelling

Gram-flour and ready made betel-bond is shown to taste his conversance in household affairs.

(m) Durvākshat Mantra – thrashed whole winnowed rice in colour & grass for well being and blessings to the couple with minimum 05 married men under head-caps.

Mantra- Om Aabhrāhman Brāhmano .... Mitranā-mudyastava- tenor-Ogod! Our inland taught-teacher be nourished with luminance of cognition or knowledge. Our inland produces arrow-notching experts and great hero-administrators & military personnels. Our inland patrons should have milking cows (for nourishment). Oxen should be capable of carrying heavy load, horses should be fast runners, our female folk should have all positive qualities to lead our inland. Rain-falls should happen on times.Crops and herbal drugs should be ripened with flower & fruits.

Our inland should acquire new property and preserve it as safe or ensured. Condemn opponent tricks and dawn proponent wishes.

Thus blessings for long life and good luck to retain wifehood (bride).

We all know that our global society celebrates marriage rituals in pre-stalled pavilions or harbours or resorts consecrated to a deity wherein we all share in our turns. Such practice may question the sanctity of the ceremony being staled for years together. But I mean to sanctify such celebrations uttering our well-known purifying mantra-one who recalls lotus-eyed Vishnu gets purified in all conditions ins and outs.

The idea to render marriage age-old ritual in English version came to my mind to let know the age-old tradition globally. Further I appeal you all to appreciate the technical operation of angelic marriage ritual sincerely.

Marriage Materials

1. Dālā – a bamboo-made round tray.
2. Supervision (groom) –
    (a) Small wooden stool
    (b) Wooden sandal
    (c) Femi-performer of rites
    (d) Customary femi-singers
    (e) Potter water jar decorated with mango leaves. Mud-made rifter to delete confusing communication
    (f) Vaka-beware of crane or hypocrite to ward off undue Clutches in symbolic mud-made
    (g) Cunning – crane-bird.
    (h) Muja-grass string, betel leaves
    (i) Tortoise skull
    (j) Vesan-gram flour

(3) Ulukal – Ukhar – wooden mortar used for cleansing rice from husk

(b) musal – wooden long shaped club with round iron bracelet fixed to one end for thumping away rice.

(4) A customary manual threshing device to extract the grain from ears of paddy.

(5) Barber

(6) Yagyopaveet – sacred thread.

(7) Kush-grass-ring

(8) Yellowish waist-cordon lace

(9) Blanket seat

(10) Conch

(11) Unbroken rice.

(12) Sandal wood

(13) Honey-mixed with curd etc.

(14) Kush-straw blades

(15) 05 whole nuts

(16) 05 whole turmeric raw material

(17) Paddy

(18) Remuneration

(19) Dhoti 04 pairs

(20) Potter-jar full of unsteamed white rice

(21) Sruva-wooden ladle

(22) Bronze dish

(23) Ghee (butter)

(24) Mango dried stalks

(25) Lāzā – popped corn of paddy denoting splendor, radiance, riches, affection, peace and etc.

(26) Rectangular bamboo open-tray for popped corn store while oblation into the Fire.

(27) Purahar- a small potter pitcher or carafe

(28) Pātil – earther belly-basin or potter round deep cup with earthen-coloured cap to half-cover the lamp.

(29) Potter-elephant decorated

(30) Praneeta patra – potter pot having shraw thread for consecration.

(31) Paita – Strāw-thread of kush grass

(32) Orange red colour vermilion/brighted colour vermilion.

The Content

Chapter – 1

MĀTRIKĀ PUJĀ
(Pre-wedding rite)

MATRIKA is Divine mother having magical power.

She has 8 or 7 or 16 manifestations as –

Brahmi, Maheswari, chandi, vārāhi, vaishnavi, kumari, chāmundā & charchikā.

Again pārvati – daughter of Himalaya mountain – sati in her former birth.

Padmā – Laxami-goddess of fortune or Vishnu consort.

Shachi – wife of Indra

Medha – a form of saraswati (Intelligence)

Sāvitri – Consort of the Brahma

Jayā – Goddess durga or victress

Devasenā – Army of gods or personified wife of skanda.

Swadhā – Fire god oblation to the Manes

Swāhā – The wife of Agni god – exclamatory oblation to the fire

Maruti – Divine mother

Lokmātar – Universal mother – epithet of laxami

Hrishti – goddess of delight

Pushti – Mother of contentment or acquiescence

Ātmakuladevata – tutelary deity.

Shreeh – Laxami being mother of riches or affluence.

Resolution – taking tri-kuch-grass, sesame and holy water to utter (vajasneyi) omadya amuka (certain) month Amuka (certain) forthnight, amuka (certain) date, Amuka clan. Asyāh shree Amuka (certain-name) kumarikāyah kārayitavya vivāh karmani ganptai durga sahitāh shodasmatri raham pujayishyate.

Now paste cow-dung with sandal paste, vermilion and red clothes against the wall to arrange 03 vertical lines each of 05 goddesses with Shree goddess separately. Touch all goddesses with banana and touching to the very wall vertically rice, penta or septa times in between the lines. And utter Om vaso pavitramasi shatdhāra vashoḥ paritramasi sahasradhāraṃ, Devastwā savitā punātu vasoḥ pavitren shatadharan suptwa kāmdhukshah.

For (chhandoga) utter-

Evamutyam Madhchyatam shatadhāram vrishabhaṃ Divo Duhaṃ vishwāvasooni vibhratam,

Sahasradhāram vrishabham payoduhaṃ priya devāya janma

Riten Ritajāto vivāvridha Rājā Deoritam Brihat.

Next to allow the deities invoked going back to their abode by Uttering – Om Ganapati Durgasahitāḥ Shodashmataraḥ pujutaḥsathāh kshamadhwaṃ swsthanaṃ Gachhataḥ.

Next offer remuneration to the priest uttering – Omadya kritaitad genapatidurgashreesahit shodash matri pujan karma pratishthḥartham etāvad dravya mulyak Hiranyamagni daivataṃ yathānām (certain) gotrāy Brahamāy dākshināmahaṇ dade.

Chapter – 2

Cow Gifting (pre-wedding rite)

After Mātrika puja the maid-gifter sitting east face taken with incense, sandal paste flower & unbroken unsteamed rice recites – Om Etāvat dravyamulyak (estimated value of an average cow) gavai namaḥ and on kusha grass – Om Brahmanāya namaḥ thrice.

Further (Vajasneyji + Chhandoga) taking kush-grass, sesame, holy water maid gifter utters – Omadya Amuke (certain) month Amuke (certain) fortright, Amuke Tithou (date certain) Amuka gotrāyāḥ Asyāh shree Amuka (certain name) kumārikāyāḥ Kārayitavya vivāh karmani prapta rajodarshan suchita Arishta Nirāsdwara Shreeparmeshwar prityartham etavata Drayamulyak (ready coins) Gāmekām Rudradaivatām Yathanām gotrāya (certain clan name) Brahmanāya Ahaṃ dade.

The maid gifter offers remuneration to the priest – Omadya kritaitad Godānpratisthartham etavatadravyamulyaka Hiranyamagni Daivatam Yothanām Gotrāya Brahmanāya (Certain name of the Brahman Clan) dakshināmahandade.

Chapter – 3

Poogādidanam
Catching hands of the bride as acceptance (pre-wedding rite)

Now the maid gifter sitting west ward utters – Om Tasmin Kāle Agni Sannidhye snataḥ snāte hayarogini. Ayange apatite Aklibe pitā tubhyam pradāsyati. Shree Amuka (Certain name of the bride Kanyām.

Next the bride mates offer grass & unbroken unsteamed rice to the groom utters–Om Ritastha Ritāvridh Ritushthastha Ritāvridhaḥ. Rritashchuto virago Nakāmdudhā Akshiyamanaḥ to be applied on his forehead.

Next the bride gifter or any senior person authorised offers sari, petticoat and allied attire to the bride uttering – Om Yā Akrintannavayam yā Atanvata yāshcha Devistantoonbhito talantha. Tāstvā Dovirajase Sanvayayaswayushmateedam paridhatsava Vāsah. Etc.

Again utters – Om Jaranganchha paridhastva Vāso Bhavakrishtee Nāmabhi Shastipāvā. Satan cha jeeva sharadaḥ survarchchā rayi cha putananusavyaya swayushmatidaṇ paridhatsva vāsaḥ.

Chapter – 4

Groom Supervisional rite

Ritual items collected:-

(i) Eaten betel by the bride for the groom.

(ii) Wooden sandal

(iii) Potter water-jar with mango leaves on the crown.

(iv) Mud-made rifter.

(v) Vaka-hypocrite-bird (Mud made.)

(vi) Banana budding leaves

(vii) Gram flour

(viii) Kush grass string

(ix) Lit-up lamp in tortoise skull.

All the above be kept in coloured-bamboo-round-deep tray. After cross-supervising such items be shown with the groom to assess his expertise in household affairs by the female-mates, they receive and escort the groom taking her tittle fingerknot with the bride to the courtyard near the Altar erected.

Chapter – 5

Leaflet bracelet – binding process

8 – Brahmanas or noble fellows with groom catch hold of wooden round – long shaped club with iron bracelet fixed to one end and thrust into the wooden deep mortar thrice and in each thrusting turn utter figurative traits of Lord Vishnu's cosmic vision – Om Sahasra Shirshā purasah Sahasrakshah Sahasrapāt. Sa Bhumigvan sarvataspritvā Atayatishthad dashānglum. Purusha Eve da gvam sarvamyat Bhutam yachabhāvāyam. Utāmritatvasya Eshāno yadannenātirohati. Etavānasya Mahimano Jyāyānshcha purukshah. Pāde Asya Vishwā Bhutāni Tripādyamritam Divi. Tripadoordha udait purushah padosyeha-bhavatpunah. Tato Vishwanga Vyakrāmat sāshanānashane Abhi. Tato viradajāyat virajoadhipurushah. Sa Jato Atyarichyat pashachād Bhumimatho purah. Tasmāt yagyāt sarvahutah sambhritam prishadāyam. Pashunstānchakre vāyavyā Nārāyanyā Grāmyāshcha je. Tasmāt yagya sarvahutah Richah sāmāni yagyire. Chhandagvansi yagyire Tasmād yagustasmāt Ajāyata. Tasmādashwā Ajāyanta ye ke chobhayādatah. Gāvo hi yagjire Tasmāt Tasmajjātā Ajāvayaḥ. Tam yagyam Barhishi praukshan purushaṃ Jātamagrataḥ. Ten Devā Ayajanta Sādhyā Rishayashcha ye. Yat purushaṃ vyadadhuḥ katidha vyakalpayaṃ. Mukhaṃ kim asyaseet kimbhāhoo kimuroopādā uchyete. Brāhmano Asya mukhamāseed Bāhuraganyaḥ kritaḥ. Ooru Tadasya yad vaishyaḥ padbhyāgvaṃ shudro Ajāyat. Chandramā Manaso Jātash chakshoḥ suryoajāyat. Shotrād Vāyashcha prānāshcha mukhādagni-Ajāyat. Nāvyā

Aaseedantarikshagvam Sheershanoḥ dyouh Samavarttat. Padabhyām Bhumisdishaḥ Shrotrāttathālokān Akalpayah. Ten purushan havishā deva yagyamatanvat. Vasanto Asyāseed rājayam grishma idhamaḥ saraddhaviḥ Saptāsyāsan paridhayastrih sapta samidhaḥ kritā deva yadyagvam tanvānā Abadhnaṇ purusham pashuṃ. Yagyen yagyamajanta devāstāni Dharmāni prathamānyāsan. Te ha nākaṃ mahimanaḥ pashuṃ. Yagyen yagyamajanta devāstāni Dharmāni prathamānyāsan. Te ha nākaṃ mahimanaḥ sachanta yatra poorve sādhyāḥ santi devāḥ - 16. Here mind that the barber binds all the partners with hand made fibre.

Next all the partners cleanse all corns of rice from their husk and the groom makes wrist binding with Mango leaves inside rice fibre-bond.

Now the maid gift is proceeded

Next the bride gifter taking curd, Clarified butter, honey, Jaggery + water (Mudhuparka) to worship the groom as Lord Vishnu and the priest requests the groom to take seat Uttering – Om Vishtaraḥ pratigrihyatām responded as Om Vishtaraḥ pratigrihnāmi.

Next on reciting – Varshmosi Samānānā Mudyatāmiva Suryaḥ emaṇ tamabhitishtāmi yo mā Kashchābhidāsati. The groom places 25 kusha grass or 03 kushgrass beneath his seat.

Next the groom washes his right foot.

Now the bride donor taking grass, unbroken rice, nut, sandal paste + holy water in a conch gives to the groom who accepts it a offerings

Next the bride donor takes a little of the components and pours on the head of the groom and the rest is thrown to its E-N Corner.

Now the priest requests the bride donor to perform rinsing his own lips with the palm of his right hand one time on reciting – Aamāgam yashasā sagvan Srija varchsā tam Mā kuru priyan pragānāmadhipatim pashunāmrishtiṃ tanoonāṃ. And later on 2 – time rinsing sans Mantras.

Next bride donor takes Madhuparka as palm covering in Bronze dish or bowl by hand reciting to the groom – Madhuparka (components alluded to above) pratigrihyatām.

Next the groom uncovers to see the Madhuparka resting in donor's hand recites – Om Mitrasya twā chakshushā prateekshe.

Now the groom on reciting – Om devasya twā savituḥ prasveashwinoḥ Bāhurbhyām pooshno hastābhyām pratigrihnāmi – takes the bowl in his left hand on next reciting – Om Namaḥ Shyāvashāya Annashane yatta Aavidhaṃ tatte Nishkrintāmi.

The groom mixes them clock-wise and pours a bit of Madhuparka with his thumb and ring finger to the ground – and reciting 02-time the sama Mantras. (Namah Shyāvā …) and pours down to the earth.

Again the groom tastes a bit of Madhuparka 03-time on reciting – Om Yanmadhuno Madhvyaṃ parmagvaṃ Rupamahhādyam. Tenāhaṃ Madhuno Madhavyena paramena Rupenānnādyena paramo Madhavyo Annādosāni. And repeats the same thricely.

Again on reciting – Om Vānma Aasyeastu – the groom touches his lips with his 05-finger.

Again the groom on reciting – Nasorme prānoastu – touches his nostrils with his thumb + ring finger to inhale life air. Again the groom on reciting – chaksorme chakshurastu – touches his eyes with his thumb + ring finger to see well.

Again the groom on reciting karnayorme shrotamastu-touches ears to hear clearly.

Again on reciting – Bahvorme Balmastu- touches his arms to have strength.

Again on reciting – Arishtāni Mengāni Tanoostanvā me sah santu – touches with his both hands from head to the toes.

Again the barber speaks – Gaurgourgourh – and lets keep a blade of kush straw (trin) in groom's hand and the groom breaks the trin and untie the trin-knot around the neck of the adjacent cow standing beside them (altar). The (chhandog) groom utters prajapatih Rishiḥ Brihatichhando Gaurdevatā purvavadhhagomokshane viniyogaḥ. Om Munch gām varunapashāda duripantam me Abhidhehi. Tam Jahyamushya chobhayoh utsriga gāmattu trināni pibatoodakam.

&

Prajapatih Rishi Strishtupchhando Gaurdevatā Gauranumantrane Viniyogaḥ : Om mātā Rudrānām duhita vasoonām swasā Aadityā nāmmritasya Nāvih. Panuvācham chikitushe janāya mā Gāmnāgamaditim vadhishthah.

Chapter – 6

Hom (oblation to the Fire) Vājasaneyi

Ahead procedure stands for Vajasaneyi

The groom sheds off one hand square land with kushgrass and throws it to the E+N corner.

Next the groom makes 03-vertical line in parallel with Sruva (a wooden ladle with triangular cup-head used for pouring clarified butter on sacrificial fire) root.

Next measures the length with span of fore-finger and thumb in one after the other style and picks out a bit of earth with fore-finger and thumb.

Next sprinkles the spot with holy water and install fire out of bronze dish in ownward turn ahead. Then the groom inflames the fire with mango or palash wooden fuel.

After that the bride-mates fetch or bring the bride from mirthful décor-room of festivity (kohavar).

After that the groom provides new sari & ornamental attire reciting – Om Jaraṇ Gachha paridhatswa vāso Bhavā-krishteenām Abhishastipāvā. Shatam cha geeva sharadaḥ suvarchā Rayim cha putrananusam vyayswā yushima-teedaṃ paridhatswa vāsoh.

Om yā Akritannvayam yā Atanvat yāshcha Devi-Astantoonabhito tatanth. Tāstwā Devirajarse samvyavaswā yushmatidam paridhalswa vāsaḥ.

The groom on reciting – Om paridhasye yasho dhasyai deerghāyatwaya Jardashtirasmi. Shataṃ chajivāmi Sharḍaḥ puroochi Rāyaspokham Abhisamvyayishye – accepts dhoti (customery attire) & etc for his own dress.

Now arrange for cross appearance between the bride and the groom mutually before entering into holy wedlock. Then the couple wash their own mouths.

Now the femi-performer lets unveil the appearance of the bride (then curtain system) reciting – Om Samanjantu Vishwedevā Samāpo Hridayani nou. Sanmātarishwā sandhātā samudeshtri dadhatu nou. And the bride donor fastens the edges of both Dhoti & Sari as the knot of nativity.

Or (Chhandoga)

The groom places near himself water-filled pot with kusha grass. And starts-

(a) Minding yellow coloured earth places his left hand on earth marking line of 12 fingers northward.

(b) Minding the Fire-god reddish coloured marks the west of the adjacent line of 21 fingers towards northword.

(c) Minding dark – coloured prapāpati (Brahma) between adjacent to the northward line and ahead of east line marking of 06 fingers east ward.

(d) Minding blue coloured God Indra marking line of fingers to the distance of 06 fingers eastward.

(e) Minding white-coloured soma God marking of 06 fingers of Sexa-fingered line totalling – 51 (Divine power-holy seat representing goddesses)

In the Middle of 05 lines cast off earth to its E+N Corner at a distance of 24 fingers.

Next the groom installs the fire flaming in bronze dish ahead himself uttering – prajapatih Rishih trishtupchandah

Agnish Devatā Agni sanskāre Viniyogaḥ. Om kravyadam Agnim prahinomi dooraṃ yamrājyam Gaechhati Ripravahaḥ.

Prajapatih Rishih Brihateecchando Brihaspatih Devatā Agnisthāpane viniyogaḥ. Om Bhoorbhuraḥ swaḥ.

Next the groom prays the fire uttering – Ehaivāya – Mitaro Jātvedā devebhyo havyaṃ vahatu prajānan.

Next the bride donor recites – prapapatih Rishih Agnidevatā Brāhmopaveshane Viniyogaḥ. Om Aavasoḥ sadane seeda. Prajāpatih Rishiḥ Gāyatrcchando Vishnurdevatā Jape Niniyogaḥ. Om idamvishnurvichakrame tredhānidadhe padam Samoodhmasya pānsule.

Mind that the young & stout one keeps standing with decorated Pitcher on his shoulder till ablutional batching as Coronation.

Next the groom takes hold of her tittle finger (unfixed attachment) from the room of festivity and the couple sits before the fire-altar eastwardly.

Kushandikā (Since Fire installation to oblation process)

(i) There are 05-type of land purification or sacra-mentation

(ii) Land purification by warding off worms with kush sweeping.

(iii) Anointing with Cow dung

(iv) Lineal engraving in 03 – erection with shruva root.

(v) Picking away earth out of lineal engraving and throw them (03 lines) to the E-N Corns

Sprinkling with holy water.

So the groom sweeps away the spot north side uttering – Kautsa Rishih Jagaleecchando Agnirderata prishtasya shadahasya pashtheahah Agni marute shaste parisamuhane viniyogah.

Om emaṃ stomamarhate Jatvedase Rathmiva Sammahemā Maneeshayā. Bhadrā hi naḥ pramatirasya samsad. Agne sakhye mārishāmā vayantava.

Next the groom sweeps away the spot east side of the Altar uttering. –

Om Bharomedhamaṃ krinavāmā haveenshi te chintyantah parvnā parvanā vayaṃ. Jivātame pratarām sādhayā dhiyagne sakhye mārishāmā vayantava,

Next the groom sweeps away right side of the Altar uttering –

Om Shaken twā samidhaṃ sādhayā Dhiyaste Devā havirandayanti Aahutam. Twamādityāṃ

Aavahatām hyushmasyagne sakhye mārishāmā vayantava.

And does scattering about or around the Altar by plenty of kushas.

Next the groom takes 20 palash (Butea Monosperma) 's small stalks and soaks their Middle ends with ghee and oblating them into the Fire silently.

Again utters mantra – prajapatih Rishih Pavitre devate paritracchedane viniyogah. Om pavitrestho vaishnovyo. Prajāpatih Rishih pavitre devate pavitra Sammārjane Viniyogah. Om Vishnohmansā putesthaḥ.

Again sprinkles water uttering – prajapatih Rishih Rajyam devatā Ajyotpavane Viniyogah. Om devastwā Savitā utpunātvachhidren pavitrena vaso suryashma Rashmibhiḥ.

Again water-fall while uttering – prajapatih Rishih Aditih devatodakāngali prasechane viniyogaḥ. Om Adite Anumanysva.

Again arrage water fall northwardly uttering – prajapatih Rishiḥ

Anumati devatodakangali prasechane viniyogah, Om Aneemate Anumanyaswa.

Next eastwardly uttering – pratapatih Rishih Saraswati-

Devatodakānjali prasechane viniyogah, Om Saraswati Anumanyaswa.

Next sprays water around the Altar uttering – prajapatih

Rishih trishtupa chhandaḥ savitādevatā Agniparyukshane Viniyogah. Om Devasavitaḥ prasuvayagyam prasuva yagyapatin bhagāya. Divyo Gandharvaḥ ketapooh ketannah punātu vācaspatih vāchannaḥ swadatu.

Next taking flower, nut and one 6" dried branch stalk of Mango or palash in groom's left hand to hold at its one end and the upper part of the stalk with right hand recites- parmeshthi Rishee rudrarupaḥ Agnish Devata Viroopākshajape Viniyogaḥ. Om tapasheha tejashchā Shradhā cha Hrishcha satyandha Akrodhashcha tyāgasheha Dhritishcha Dharmashcha satvanch Vākcha Manshacha Aatmācha Brahma Cha Tāni prapadly tani Mānvantu. Bhoobhuraḥ swaro Mahāntamātmānam prapadye. Viroopākshosi Dautagistasya te shayyāparne. Grihāntarikshe Vimitam hiranyamayam tatadevānām ttridgāni Ayamasmaye kumbhe Antaḥ Sannihitāni Tāni Balbhriccha Balsāccha Rakshatopramanie Animishate tatsatyam yatte dwādesh putraste twā samvatsare Samvatsare Kāmaprena yagyen jājayitvā punaḥ Boahmavaryam upayanti twan Deveshu Brahmah Asyaham Manushyeshu Brāhmno vai Brahmanan updhavatyuptwā Dhāvāgni Japayanta Mā Mā pratijāpi Jurhantam Mā Mā pratihousheeh kurvantaṃ Mā Mā pratikārshistwām prapadhye twayāgrasoot idamkarma karishyāmi. Tanme Radhyatām Tanme samridyatām tanme uppadyatām samudro mā viswavyachā Brahmā nujanātu tuthomā vishwaveda Brahmanaḥ putronuganātu shwatroma pracheta Maitravaruno- Janātu. Tasmai viroopakshāya. Dantāngaye samudrāya vishwavyachse tuthaya vishwavedase shwātrāya prachetase sahastrakshāy Brahmanaḥ putrāya namaḥ.

And cast it off to the N + E Corner.

Next the groom gives fruits and flower to the Brahmā personified and offers stalk oblation to the Fire uttering the same aforesaid mantra.

Next the groom offers oblation with ghee kept in Shruva to the Fire reciting – prajapatih Rishih gāyatricchando Agnih Devata Vyahritihome viniyogah. Om Bhooswāhā ....(1)

Prajapatih Rishih ushnikacchandah vāyardevata vyāhritihome viniyogah. Om Bhuvaḥ swānā ...(2)

Prajapatih Rishih Anush tupcchandah savitā Devata Vyahritihome viniyogah; Om Swaḥ swānā ...(3)

Prajapatih Rishih Brihaticchandaḥ Brihaspatirdevata Mahāvyahritinome Viniyogaḥ; Om bhoorbhuvaḥ swaḥ swāhā ...(4)

Next the groom lets touch her right arm with his right hand offering oblation into the fire uttering (06 times) prajapatih rishih ratijagateecchandah Agnirdevatā Ajyāhutau Viniyogah – Om Agniretu Prathamo devatābhyah Sosye prajammunchahi Mrityupashāta. Tadayam Rājā varuno Anumanyatām yatheyam stree poutramagham Na Rodāt Swāhā ...(1)

Prajapatih Rishih Jagateecchando Agnidevatā Aajyahutou viniyogah. Om imam Agnish trāyatām gārhpatyah praja-Masmai Jardishtam krinotu. Ashunyopasthā Jivatāmastu Mātā poutramanandam Abhi Vibudyatām iyam swāhā. ...(2)

Prajapatih Rishih shakkaricchandaḥ Viswedevadevata Ajyahutou viniyogah. Om dyoste prishtham rakshatu Vayu Roo Roo ashwinou cha. Stanandhyāste putranutsavitābhi Rakshatvāvāsasah paridhanāt Brihaspatih Vishwedevā Abhirakshantu pashchat Swātā. ...(3)

Prajapatih Rishih Ratijagateecchando agnyādayo devatā Ajya hutao viniyogah. Om Mā te griheshu Vishi gosha utthādamyatra twadrudatyaḥ samvishantu mā twam roodayuraḥ Aavadhishthā givapatni patiloke virajam pasyantee prajā sumansyamānām Swāhā ...(4)

Prajapatih Rishih uprishtata Brihaticchando Agnyadayo devatā Ajujāhutau Viniyogah. Om Aprajasyam poutramartyam pāshmanmuta vā Adham. Sheershnaḥ srajmivonmuchya dwishadbhayah pratimunchāmi pāsham swāhā. .... (5)

Prajapatih Rishih Atyushnikcchandah Vaivaswatodevatā Agyahutou viniyogah. Om paraitu Mrityramritam Aagāt vaivaswto no Abhayam krinotu. Parmmrityonuparchi pantha yatra no Anya itaro devayanāta. Chakshushmato Shrinvate te Braveemi mā nāh prajām Rorishomota veerāntaswāhā. ...(6)

In the long run untie leaflet bracelet and knot of nativity.

Chapter – 7

Bride gifting (Vājasaneyi)

The couple sits to the west side of the Fire-God on herbal matron and lets the bride be seated to his right side.

Next the groom provides flower, sandal paste, betel and customary dress materials to the Brahma personified being relevant & honourable relative or symbolic kush-made Brahma on uttering – Om Adya kartavya Vivāhānghom karmani kritā-kritavekshan rupa Brahmakarma Kartum certain Gotra certain Sharmānaṃ Brahmanam Ebhih pushpa chandan Tambul Jagyopaveet Vāsobhih Brahmatvena tvāmahaṃ vreene.

And the groom requests the Brahmā to be seated on moving clock-wise around the Fire-God reciting – Om asmin karmani twan me Brahma bhava – responded as Bhavāni. And the Brahma taking his dress Materials utters-vritosmi. Again the groom speaks to the Brahma – Yathā Vihitam karma kuru and the Brahma responds – Karvāni.

And the Brahma be seated on the south side of the flaming Fire-God.

Afterwards the groom places pre-filled-potter-water wrapped with kush grass to the north side of the Fire-God.

Next kushandika (Since Fire installation to oblation process)

64 tri-bladed kush-grass taken to spread around 04 sides of the Fire-God as – N+E Corner = 16

Brahma to the Fire God = 16

S+W corner to the W+N Corner = 16

Fire God to pre filled potter pot = 16

Now having 03 kush-grass to the N+W side

02 blades of Kush-grass having their roots

Wooden sacrificial Ladle, Cowghee pot, 256 fistful of organic unsteamed rice (remuneration for the Brahma) in potter-pot be placed serially.

Chapter – 8

(Vajasaneyi) Popped corn rice of the paddy oblation to the Fire

Next arrange grass-mixed popped rice of paddy, stone piece, brother of the bride, bamboo conoidal broth, barber, wooden fuel material for sacrificial oblation and the like.

Next break 02-blade of kushagrass to form paita (straw-thread) and placing potter pot for holy water consecration to the Fire God by prayers and catching the straw thread (paita) with thumb + ring finger and spray such water thrice on his (groom) own head.

Now taking prokshni pot in his left hand and catching paita with his ring + thumb fingers of his right hand – spray such water thrice on his own head and spray all rite's materials and place prokshani pot near Fire God + praneetā Pot.

Next heat the ghee pot on fire and let moved by the groom around the ghee – pot with straw-thread (paita) and throws it into the fire.

Next placing kusha grass down the Fire-Marrying in his (groom) left hand minding the prajapati God and soaking 03 wooden stalks measuring thumb+fore finger span to throw them into the fire-flames.

Now spray with prokshani pot-water into the fire and pup up the paita (a blade of straw-kusha) loosing down his right thigh to connect himself to the Brahma with Kush-grass.

Further groom recites 12 montras (sacred formula) and in each Mantra pours ghee with ghee-kept sruva and the rest of ghee-drops be sprayed into prokshani pot as:-

Om prajapataye Swāhā, idam prajapataye ...(1)

Om idrāya swāhā idnindrāyā ...(2)

Om Agnaye Swāhā idmagnaye ...(3)

Om Samāyaswāhā idamsomāyā ...(4)

Om Bhooh swāhā idaṃbhooh ...(5)

Om Bhuvaḥ Swāhā idaṃbhuvaḥ ...(6)

Om Swaḥ Swāhā idaṃ swaḥ ...(7)

Om twanno Agne varunasya vidwān Devasya

Hedo Avayāsiseeshtā. Yagishtham Vahnitamaḥ

Shoshuchano Vishwādweshāngwansi pramumugdhyasmāt & wāhā, idamagnee varunābhyām ...(8)

Om sa twanno Agne Avamo Bhavo teene Dishto Ashyā ushaso vyushtou. Avayakshva no Varuna gwan Rarāno

Breehi Mreedeekgwam Suhavo Na edhih Swāhā, idmagni varunābhyām ...(9)

Mayā Asi. Ayāno yagyam vahāsyayāno dehi Bheshapagwam Swāhā idmagnaye ...(10)

Om ye te shatam varuna ye sahasram yagyiyāh pasha vitatā Mahāntah. Tebhirnno-Adya Savitoat Vishnurvishwe Munchantu Marutah swarkkāh swāhā, idam varunāya savitre vishnave vishwebhyo Devebhyo Marudbhyaḥ Swarkkebhyaḥ. ...(11)

Om uduttamavvarunaḥ pāshmasmad Avādhamaṃ vimadhya-Magwan shrathaya – Athāvayamāditya Broote tavānāgaso Aditaye syām swāhā, idaṃ varunāya ...(12)

On touching holy water the groom recites –

Om vāyurantrikshasya Adhipati Samāvatva Asmin

kshetrasyāmā Rikshyasyām purudhayaṃ Agmien karmanasyām devahutyagwan swāhā, idam vāyave Antarikshasya adhipataye.

Om Suryo devedhipatiḥ *samā* vatwasmin Brahmanyasnin Kshetrasya Āmāshishyāsyāṃ purodhāyam asmin karman Asyām devahutwagvam swāhā, idam suryāya Divo Adhipataye.

Om Chandra Nakshatrānāṃ Adhipatih Samāvata Asmen Brahmanyashim kshetrasaya Āmāshishya Asyam purodhāyām Asmin karmani Asyām Devahutvām swāhā.

Idam chandramase Nakshatrānām adhipataye.

Om Brihaspati Brahmano adhipatih Samāvatvasmin Brahanyasamin kshetrasyām Ashishyām purodhayām Asmin karmanasyām devahutāgwan swāhāh, idam Brihaspataye Brahmanodhi-pataye.

Om Mitrah satyānam Adhipatih Samāvatvasmin Brahmanyasmina kshetrasyām Ashishyām purodhāyām Asmin karmanasyām devahutyāgwan swāhā, idam Mitrāy satyanāmadhipataye.

Om varunopamadhipatih….

Om Samudrah srotyānāmadhipatiḥ….

Om Annagvam sāmrājya….

Om Soma oghadhināmadhipatih….

Om Savitā prasavānampatih….

Om Rudraḥ pashoonāmadhipati….

Again touch water of the praneetā pot uttering –

Om param Mreetyo Anuparehi pantha yaste Anyaitaro Devayānāt. Chakshushmate Shreenvane te Bravomi Mānan prajāgvam reerisho not veerān swāhā, idam Mreetyave.

Now the groom standing takes his bride ahead being eastward and both start moving with hollowed palms of both hands together as the bride places her hollowed palm of her hands upon that of the groom – and the brother of the bride pours popped corn of paddy mixed with shami leaves + ghee on her palm and again continues lāvā (popped corn of pady) giving (1/3 portion) into her palm while the couple moving around the fire-Altar uttering-

Om aryamanaṃ Devaṃ kanyā Agnim Ayakshata. Sa No Aryamā Devaḥ preto Munchatu Mā pateḥ swāhā, idmarya Mane.

Again the brother of the bride pours ½ of the Lava-reciting – Om iyam Nāryapabrute Lājānāvapantika Aayushmān Astu Me patired hantām gyātayo mama swāhā idmagnaye.

Again pours the rest lāvā (popped corn of paddy) reciting by the priest wishing all success of her husband –

Om imānllājā Nāva pāmyagnou samridhi karnam tava. Mama Tubhyam cha samvadanam tadagnih Anumanya tāmiyam Swāhā idmagnaye.

Next the groom touching the right foot of the bride placing eastward towards the stone piece lying to the north side against the fire-altar and utters –

Om aaroho Mamashmān Ma shmeva twagvam sthira Bhava. Abhitishtha preetanyato Avabādhaswa preetnāyataḥ.

Next the bride placing her foot on the stone piece the groom recites –

Om Saraswati predamava subhage vājineevati-yantwā Vishwasya bhutasya prajāyām asyāgrataḥ. Yasyām bhutagvam vishwan idam Jagata. Tāmadya Gathān Gasyāmiyā streenam uttamanyashah.

Next the groom taking forword the bride moves around the Brahma and praneetā pot uttering –

Om tubhyama gre paryavahan suryām vahatu nā saḥ

Punah patibhyo jāyām dāgne prajayā saha.

Again popped corn of paddy oblation is repeated as referred to above thrice along circumambulation clock-wise.

In this way 3+3+3-9 times circumambulation, concatching palms while footing on the stone piece reciting Mantra stanza already referred to for the same purpose.

Lastly the bride's brother gives Lāvā on the hollowed palms of the bride and she, in standing mode, gives sacrificial oblation to the Fire-God reciting –

Om Bhagāya swāhā idam bhagāya.

At the 4th time the couple, while standing, adopts circumambulation around the Fire and next be seated.

Next the groom connects the Brahmā to himself and performs oblation with ghee into the Fire uttering –

Om pajāpataye swāhā

And again pours ghee into the prokshani pot uttering "idam prajāpataye."

Chapter – 9

Popped Corn of paddy oblation (Chhandoga)

Both systems (Vajasaneyi + Chhandoga) have the same process but differ in Mantras –

The groom recites while the foot of the bride is placed on the stone piece – praāpathh Rishih Anshtupcchandah Ashmā devatā Ashmākramone Viniyogah. Om imam Ashmānam Aarohash-Meva twan stirā Bhava. Dwishantam Apadādhaswa Mā cha twam Dwishtāmadhaḥ.

The bride placing her foot on the stone piece pefroms oblation (popped corn of paddy) Concatching both hollowed palms in up-down mode –

Prapāpatih Rishih uprishtājyotishomatee cchando Agnih Devatā. Lājahoma viniyogah. Deerghāyuh Astu Me patih शतं Varshāni Jeevatwedhantām gātayo mama swāhā. – wishing her husband life-span of century- year long.

Next the groom gets the bride moved around the fire uttering –

Prajāpatih Rishih trishtupccandaḥ kanyādevatā parinayane viniyogah. Om kanyalā pitreebhyah patilokam yateeyam Apadeekshā Mayashta. Kanyā uta twayā vayan dhārā unanyā ivātigāhemani dwishaḥ.

Again the bride offers oblation with ghee mixed lāvā into the fire uttering –

Prapapatih Rishih uparishtād Breehateechhandaḥ pushā Devatā Lājahoma Viniyogah. Om pooshannanu.

Devan kanyā Agnim Ayakshat. Sa imāṃ Devah pushā preto Munchātu Mā pate swāhā.

The 4th time the bride offers oblation with the rest of ghee mixed with lāvā into the Fire silently.

Chapter - 10

Saptapadee (07 – Step Vājasaneyi)

Here the bride and the groom move, stroll or circumambulate 07-step after which the Marriage stands immutable or irreversible.

Since prima period Aripan or ahipan refers to smearing the earth with Cow-dung and clay for fertile and fruitful land as well as its purification.

Later on as derivative to honour and invoke Gods through Rangoli used to be marked on the floor to seek their graces.

Out of 07 times each entity to step up forward conveys through Mantras-

Om ekamishe vishnustwā Nayatu ...(1)

Om dve oorje Vishnustwā Nayatu ...(2)

Om treeni Rāyasposāya Vishnustwā Nayatu ...(3)

Om Chatvāri Māyobhavāya Vishnustwā Nayatu ...(4)

Om panch pashubhyo Vishnustwā Nayatu ...(5)

Om shadreetubhyo Vishnustwā Nayatu ...(6)

Om Sakhe saptapadā Bhavsā māmmuvratā Bhava
Vishnustwā Nayatu ...(7)

Next the groom seated to the west of the fire and taking Mango leaves already installed in the water-jar.

Sprinkles over the bride uttering –

Om Aapah Shivā Shivatamāh Shāntāh Shāntatamāh

Taste kreenvantu Bheshajaṃ.

Again the groom sprinkles over the bride reciting 03 mantra

Om Aapohishta Mayobhuvastāh Na oorge dadhāfan.

Maheranāya Chakshase ...1

Om yo Vaḥ Shivatamo Rasastasya Bhāgayteh Nah.

Ushteeriva Mātaraḥ ...2

Om tasmā Arangamām vo yasya kshayāya Jinvatha Aapo

Janyathā Cha Naḥ ...3

Again he speaks to the bride – Om Suryamudeekshaswa

And the bride sees the Sun uttering.

Tachkshuriti dadhyanātharvan Rishih pur ushnika Chhandaḥ Suryo devatā tadeekshane viviyogaḥ.

In the event of the sunset the groom tells the bride to see the polar star as – omdhruvamudikshaswa.

Here the bride seeks to look at Dhruva Tara (polar star recognized near Saptarishi Constellation – straight line of 02 stars) in order to fix the current wedlock –

While the groom recites-

Om dhruvam Asi dhruvam twā pashyāmi dhruvaidhi poshye Mayi. Mahyām twādād Breehaspati. Mayā patyā prapāvatse sangleva sharadḥa shatam.

Again the groom touching her heart with his right arm/hand resting on her right shoulder utters-

Om Mama vrate te hreedayam dadhāmi, Mama chintamunuchitam te Astu. Manvācham ekamanā Jashasva prapāpatishtā

Nyunaktu Mahyam – think unanimously at heart.

He ionises the Mantra –

Om Sumangaleeriyam Vadhoorimagvam Sameta Pashyat. Soubha-Gyamasye datvā yāthāstam Vipareta na.

After that a stout maid makes the bride seated into the deco-ceremonical room on red circumcised calf skin.

Next the groom connecting the Brahmā with himself performs swishta kreet oblation into the Fire with ghee uttering –

Om Agnaye swishtakreete swāhā, idmagnaye swhishtakreete and drops the rest of ghee in the prokshani pot.

Next the groom rinsing with holy water out of the prokshani pot and taking the pre-filled potter jar offers as remuneration for the Brahma reciting-

Omadya kreetaitat vivihāngabhuta homkarmani kreetākreeta vekshana rup Brahma karma pratishthār tham idam purnapātram prajapati daivatam certain gotrāya certain sharmana (add name) Brāhmanāya Brahmane dakshinā tubhyam aham sampradade. The groom speaks – pratipādyate & responded by the Brahmā –Om swasti

But in symbolic kusha – made Brahma utter omadya…..

Brahmana dakshinā namaḥ and no response and untie the kush knot being Brahmā.

But in the case of the Brahmā personified the groom sees off the Brahma by catching his right hand around clock-wise movement.

Next the groom applies yellow or orange coloured powder (Hgs – Murcury Sulphoid) to line up in the Mid-point of her crown hair lining.

Now the groom gives remuneration to the priest uttering – omadya kreetaitad vivāhakarma pratishthārtham etāvato dravyamulyok Hiranyam Agni daivatam certain name + clan (add name of the priest) Brahmanāya Dakshinām Aham dade.

Then at least 05 Brahmins give blessing with grass + unbroken rice called durvākshat rite uttering-

Om Aabrahman Brāhmano Brahmavarchosee Jāytāmā rashtre Rājanyaḥ shoor ishavyoti Vyādhee Maharatho Jāytām dogdhree Dhenurbodha nadavānāshuh Saptih purandhriyoshā Jishnu ratheshtah sabheyo yuvāsya yagamānasya veero Jāytām Nikāme Nikame nah parjanyo vyarshatu phalvatyo na oshadhayaḥ pachyantām yogakshemo naḥ kalpatām.

Om Matrārthaḥ Siddhayaḥ santu poornāḥ santu Manorathaḥ. Shatroonāṃ Budhināshostu Mitrānām udayastava.

Next performing affectionate rite through graceful felicitation with benedictory singing by hermates. So at least 05 – female relatives in their turn, touch the couple's feet, knees, shoulders and heads offering grass and paddy as blessings. Next the female relatives lift up Dātā (full of colourned paddy, fresh curd pot, fruits, betel and nuts) and touch both's heads thrice as blessings again and thereby end such marriage rites for the time being.

Chapter 11

Saptapadi (07 – Step – Chhandoga)

Now the groom looking forward the marriage party recites – prajapatih Rishih Anushtup chhandah Ashāsyamānā Devatā Kanyāprekshaka Janānumantren viniyogah. Om Sumangleeriyam vadhoorimā samet pashyat. Soubhāgyam Asyai dattvāyāthāstam vipritena.

Next the groom sprinkles jar-water taken on shoulder of the standing young one utters-

Prapapatih Rishih Anushtupchhando viswadeva Samātariswa Samdhatree Sanudeshtrayo Devatā murddhanya Abhishechane nou. Samātarishwā Samdhātā Samudeshtree Dadhātu nou.

Next the groom catching the lower portion of her palm with the right open palm of her right hand recites-

Prajāpatih Rishih gāyatree chhando Agnirdevatā Vyāhreeti home viniyogah. Om Bhuvah Savitādevatā Vyāhreetihome viniyogah, Om swaḥ Swāhā

Prajāpatih Rishih Breehateechhando Breehaspatih Devatā Mahāvyahreeti home viniyogah; om Bhoorbhuvah Swah Swāhā

Next ending to accomplish oblation, the groom taking ghee+fruits+betels in the Sruva's head-cup utters prajapatih Rishih Virādgāyatri Chhandah indrodevatā yashaskāmasya yajaneeya prayoge viniyogha; Om poorna homaṇ Yashase juhomi yosmai juhoti varmasmai Dadāti Varaṃ Breene yashasā Bhāmi loke swāhā.

The groom gives remuneration to the Brahmā uttering-Om Adya kritaitad pānigrahan homkarmani kreetākreetā vekshakāya Brahmane idam purna pātraṃ (Rice pot) prajāpatidaivatam (certain clan of certain name of the personified Brahma be added) dakhina Namaḥ the Brahmā receives such remuneration uttering –Om Swasti.

Next purification with ashes to apply through ring finger on own heart uttering Om tryāyusham Jamadagnah.

On own right armroot – Om kashyapasya tryayusham.

On own left arm root- Om Agastya asya tryāyusham.

On own forehead – Om-yadya Devānām tryāyasham Tanme Astu trayāyusham.

Next the groom applies ashes (remains of the hom) on her bride heart & etc. in the above order reciting the same Mantras.

Chapter – 12

Post-Marriage rite (Chhandoga)

Here the procedure is the same as noted above at its relevance with different Mantras.

So repeat fire – installation pouring the straw –thread in the bronze-based dish uttering Mantras by the groom–

Prajāpatih Rishiḥ treeshtupchhandaḥ Agnirdevatā Agnishanskare viniyogah. Om kravyādamagnim prahinomi Dooram Yamirājyam Gancchatu ripravāhḥ.

Again the groom pours off the fire of the dish ahead of himself uttering – prajāpatih Rishi Breehatecchhandah Breehas patin Devatā Agnisthāpane viniyogah.

Next the groom prays the Fire uttering-

Om ihaiv Prapāpatihyamitaro Jātaveda devebhyo havyam vahatu prajānan.

And cast off the wooden stalks into the Fire silently.

Next the groom offers dress-materials to the Brahmā personified uttering – Om Asyām Ratrou Matkartavya uttarvivah homkarmani kreetakreeta vekshanrupa Brahmatwen ebhih pushpachandan tāmbool yagyopaveet Vāsobhiḥ certain gothram certain sharmānam (utter name of the Brahmā) Brahmanan twām Aham Breene – the Brahma responses as Breetosmi. The groom utters – yathāvihitaṃ karm kuru and the Brahmā responses as Om

Karvāni. Mind, here, that the Brahmā made of kush grass need not go through such responses.

Next the groom placing his right forearm upon the left one while flexing or bowing the both hands on the ground uttering –

Parmeshthee Rishiḥ Anushtupcchandah Agnidevata Bhumejape Viniyogha. Om idam Bhoomeh Bhajamah idam bhodram sumanglam parāsapatnān Bādhastwāni eshām vindate vasu.

Next the groom taking tri-kush grass in his right hand to shed off the spot recites- koutsa Rishih Jagateecchandah Agnirdevatā preethasya Shadahasy Shashthe Ahani Agnimārute Shaste parisamuhane viniyogah. Om imam stomam Arhate Jātvedase rathmiva Sammahegā Maneeshayā. Bhadrāhinah pramatirasya samsadhyagne sakhye mārishāmā vayantava. ...(1)

Om Bharomedhman keenvāmā haveenshi te chityantah parvanā parvanā vayam. Jeevātame pratarām sādhayā Diyogne sakhye mārishāmā vayantava. ...(2)

Om shakam twā samidham sādhayā dhiyaste deva havih Adantyāhutam. Twamādityā Aavahatām hyushmastyagne sakhye Mārishāmā vayantava ...(3)

Again winnow with kush-grass to the north of Fire

Again recites – om Bharomedhmaṇ kreenvāmā haveeshim te sādhaya Dhiyagne Sakhye Mārishāmā vayantava to the east of Fire – Altar.

Again recites – om shakem twā samidham sādhayā dhiyaste deva havirandanti Aahutam. Twamadityam Aavhatām hyushmagne sakhye mārishāmā vayantāva – to the south of the fire.

Again repeat as in Vajasaneyi system and recite – prajāpatih Rishih pavitre devātā pavitrasamārjane viniyogah. Om vishnoḥ Manasā pootesthaḥ.

Repeat as in Vajasaneyi system and recites-

Prajapatih Rishi Rāgyam Devatā Jyotpavane viniyogah. Om devaswā samitotpunāt Avchhidren pavitrena Vasoḥ sooryasya Rashmibhih.

Again repeat as in Vajasheyi system and recites- prajapatih Rishih Aditidevatā udkānjali prasechane viniyogah. Om adite Anumanyswa to worship the Sun.

Next let flow of holy water to the north side of the fire reciting- prajapatih Rishih Saraswati devatodkānjoli prasechane viniyogah. Om Saraswati Anumanyaswa to worship goddess of learning.

Next encircle around the Fire with water-fall reciting- prajāpathi Rishih trishtapchhandaḥ savitadevatā Agnih paryakshane viniyogah. Om devasavitah prasuva yagyam prasuva gagyapatim Bhagāya. Divyā gandharvah ketapooh ketannaḥ punātu vāchaspaith vāchannaḥ swadatu.

Again repeat the process as in vajashaneyi system to recite parmeshthi Rishee Rudrarupo Agnirdevatā Virupakshajape viniyogaḥ. Om tapasheha tegashcha shradhācha Areenshcha Satyanch akrodhashcha tyāgashcha dhreetishcha Darmashcha satwancha vākcha Manashcha Aatmācha Brahma cha tāni prapadye tāni Māmvantu. Bhoorbhuvah Swaro Mahāntana aatmānam prapadye. Virupākshosi dantāngistasya te sahyyaparane grihāntarikshe vimitam Hiranya mayaṃ taddevānām Hreedānya yasmaye kumbhe Antah sannihitāni tāni Balbhareeccha Barsāccha rakshato pramanee Animishat tatsatyam yatte dwādash putrste twā samvatsare samvatsare kāmprena yagyen gājayitwā punah Brahmacharya upayanti to twan deveshu Brāhmano Asyaham Manukshyeshu Brahman ova Brāhmano updhāvati upatwā dhāvāmi. Japanta mā mā pratijapee jurhavantam Mā Mā pratihoushoch kurvantam mā mā pratikārsheestwān prapadye twayā prasoot idam karm karishyāmi tanmeradhyatām tanme samreedyatām tanma upapadytām samudro mā vishwavyachā Brahmānu Jānātu tuthoma vishwavedā Brahmanah putronujānātu shwātroma prachetā maitrāvaruno aniyānātu. Tasmai viroopākshāya dantānjaye Samudrāy Vishwavyachase tuthāya vishwavedase shwātrāy prachetase Sahasrākshāya Brahmnaḥ putrāya namaḥ.

Again repeat the process as in vajasaneyi system and the groom offers oblation to the fire and the rest drop over bride's head 06 times with ghee as – prajapatih Rishih anushtupcchandah Kanyadevata uttar vivāhe pāni grāhasya Aajyāhome viniyogah. Om lekhā Sandhishu pakshma swāvarteshu cha yānite. Tāni te poornā-hutwā sarvāne shamayāmi ahaṃ swāhā ...(1)

Prajapatih Rishih Anushtupacchandah kanyādevatottar vivāhe pānigrāhsyajyahome viniyogah. Om kesheshe yaccha pāshakameekshite Rudite cha yat. Tani te purnā hutwa sarvani shamyāmi Aham swāhā ...(2)

Prajapati .... Viniyogah. Om Sheele yaccha pāpaka Bhāshite hasitecha yat. Tānite poornāhutwā.... Swāhā ....(3)

Prapapatih ... Viniyogah. Om aarokeshu chadanteshu hastayoḥ pādyoshcha yat. Tānite ... Swāhā ...(4)

Prajapati ... viniyogah. Om oorvorupasthejanghyoh sandhāneshu cha yāni te. Tanite ... swāhā ... (5)

Prajapatih ... viniyogah. Om Yāni kāni cha ghorāni Sarvāngeshu tavābhavan poorhahutibhi Rajyasya sarvāni tāni Asheeshamaṃ swāhā ...(6)

Next the couple standing near the fire-Altar, the groom shows the polar star to the bride reciting- prajāpatih Rishi Dhruvo devatā Dhruva darshane viniyogah. Om dhruvam Asi dhruvāham patikule bhooyāsaṃ shree (utter name of the groom) Sadā shree (utter name of the bride) Sharmadā for stable couple attachment.

Next the bride sees Arundhati star (an emblem of marital commitment or constancy and counsel) whispering – prajapatih Rishiḥ Vadhoordevatā Arundhati Darshane viniyogah. Om Arundhatyasi Roodhāhmasmi.

Next the groom touching the bride's body slightly consecrates her by uttering –

Prajapatih Rishih Anushtupcchandah Kamyādevata Kanyānumantrane viniyogah; Om dhruvā dyou Dhroovā prithvee dhruram Vishwamidam jagat. Dhruvāsaḥ parvatā ime dhruvā stree patikule iyam. – wishing the relationship as stable as the earth.

Next the bride uttering her own name, clan and thread knot of nativity offers obeisance or reverential salutation to the groom.

After that Mango stalks of fore finger + thumb span be cast off/ thrown into the fire.

Next encircle the Fire Altar with water-fall uttering – prajāpatih Rishih trishtupchhandah Savitādevatā Agnih paryukshane viniyogaḥ. Om devasitahaḥ prasurajagyam pratuva ya gyapatim Bhagāya Divyo Gandharva Ketapuḥ keṭannaḥ punatu vāchannaḥ swadatu.

Now pour water having eastward face to the south of the Fire-Altar uttering – prajāpatih Rishih Aditih Devatodakanjali prasechane viniyogah. Om adite Anvamansthāḥ.

Again north ward face to the west of the Fire-altar uttering – repeat the above Mantra as prapapah.... Asthā.

Again eastward face to the north of the Fire Altar uttering – prapāpatih Rishih Saraswati devalodakāngali prasechane viniyogaḥ. Om Saraswati Anvamansthā.

Now picking up all Kushas (used) into a bundle to soak with ghee and sprinkling holy water to cast off the bundle into the fire uttering –

Prajāpati Rishih Anushtupcchando Rudro devatā Darvagutikā home viniyogah; Om Yaḥ pashoonām Adhipatee Rudrastaṃ ticharo pashoonasmākam Mā hinseeretadastu Hutam tava Swāhā.

The groom concludes oblation into the Fire with Shruva (wooden ladle) + ghee + fruits + Betel + Nut + flower by casting off into the Fire uttering –

Prajapati Rishih Virād Gāyatrichhandaḥ indro-vatā yashaskāmasya gajaneya prayoge viniyogah; impurnahomam yashase juhomi yah asmai juhoti varmasmai dedāti varaṃ vreeha yashasā Bhā mi loke swāhā. Again pour excess of shee into the Fire-altar uttering – Om Vasubhyaḥ Swāhā.

Now the groom applies purifying touch with ashes (remains of hom) through ring finger himself and the Bride uttering – trayāyushanjamdegne – to hearts.

Om Kasyapasya + rayāyusham – to right arm – root.

Om Agastyasya trayāyusham – to left arm root.

Om yad devānām trayāyusham tanme (but "tatte" for bride) Astu trayāyusham – to foreheads.

Now the groom offers remuneration to the Brahmā with filled-up rice-pot uttering –

Om Adya kreetaitad uttarvivāhkarma pratishtārtham etavadhravya mulyaka (addd cow-valued coins-certain amount) Gāmekām Rudradaivatām yathānamgotrāy Dakshinām Aham dade.

Now as noted earlier Durvākshata rite is done for the blessed couple.

Lastly graceful felicitation with rice-paddy, curd, fruits, betel, nut in a bamboo casket is observed and a bit of curd is applied to the couple cheeks by some senior reative wishing promising coronation togetherly.

Chapter – 13

Quadrantal rite (Vājasaneyi system)

The couple should pass over 03 nights since 1st Marriage day in celibacy and sacrament rather together-living. And on the 4th day the couple should bathe on pālo (horizontal plough joints on the neck of the animal) at dawn time in the courtyard and enters into the room of festivity (koutukāgār).

Next the groom spreads kushas to sweep away and throws them to N+E corner. Further smear the spot with Cow-dung.

Erect 03 vertical lines measuring each span of fore finger + thumb upwardly.

The groom picks up earth out of the Middle of each – 03 line and sprinkles holy water on the spot.

Again the groom taking mango flaming stalks of 6-7" and installs the fire-stock.

Next the groom takes solemn vow on reciting –

Om Ashyām Ratrou Kartavya-Chaturthi hom Karmani kreetā-kreetā vekshanrupa Brahma Karmkartum … clan … sharma (speak name of the groom) Brahmanṃ ebhiḥ pushpa chandan tāmbool yagyopaveet vāsobhiḥ Brahmatwan twāmaham Breene.

The Brahma replies – Breetosmi and the groom speaks to the Brahmā – yathā vihitam kar kuru-further replied by the Brahmā – Om karvāni.

Or mind here that kush-grass-made Brahma or the Brahma personified be seated moving or let move around the fire Altar clock wise to the north side of the Fire-Altar.

A preethuda (a potter vessel for boiling rice + barley or the life for presentation to the God and the Manes) be placed by the groom to his north side.

Next pup-upahead praneetā pot filled with holy water covered kushas roughly. This praneeta pot is kept to his north side also.

Further as told earlier 16 kushas be used for scattering about the Altar from south to east corner, 16 kushas from the Brahmā to the Fire-Altar, 16 Kushas south to north corner and Next the groom places 03 – tri-kusha to his N+W side.

Next devise paita (upper parts of 02 bades of Kusha-grass) + 256 fistful of white unsteamed rice be collected with wooden fuel, 03 stalks, Cow ghee, Shruva, Charuka pot (boiled rice pot).

Next the groom takes in paita and sprinkles water into prokshani pot thrice – takes that upper 02 parts (paita) with his fore finger and thumb and sprinkles on his head-crown.

Next taking prokshani pot in his left hand with paita sustaining through ring finger + thumb of his (groom) right hand.

Next to spray on his crown slightly and sprinkles all ritual commodities and the groom places prokshani pot between the Fire-Altar & praneetā pot.

Next the groom washes off that charu (rice boiled) and pours it into ghee pot and places that charu pot to the north side of the Fire-Altar.

Next the groom places that ghee pot to the south of the Fire-Altar.

Next the groom makes moved around the Fire.

Next the groom warms the Sruva thrice.

Next the groom sweeps away the Sruva from root to its end of inward side and sprays holy water on it.

Next the groom warms that rice thrice and palces it near by.

Now detach the charu pot trom the Fire and place it to the north side of the ghee pot.

Next sprinkle the ghee on his (groom) head and unwanted material in the ghee be replaced, if seen.

Again sprinkle prokshani water on his head.

Next the groom takes marrying kush (Virani) with left hand minding it prajāpati (god presiding over Creation) and soaks the wooden stalks into the ghee and throws them into the fire silently.

Next the groom sprays the Fire with prokshani water in a round way and places the paita in prokshani pot while leaning his right thigh and connects himself with the Brahmā through Kushas-grass.

Next the groom offers oblation with ghee cuped Sruva into the Fire reciting – Om prajāpataye swāhā and at the same time cast off the rest drops of ghee into prakshani pot.

The groom retains the process – "Om indrāya" namah into the Fire and recites – "idam indrāya" into prokshani pot.

Again retains the process reciting "Agnaye swāhā" into the Fire and "idmagnaye" in to the prokshani pot.

Again the groom recites – "somāya swāhā" into the Fire and "idam somāya" into prokshani pot.

Now disconnect with the Brahmā and throw away ghee into preethud pot (pot glowing like Agni) reciting 05 Mantras in turns –

Om Agne pryashchitte twan devānām prāysh chittarasi

Brahmanestwā Nāth kām updhāvāmi yā Asyai patighnee tanoostām Asyai nāshaya swāhā idmagaye …(1)

Om vāyo prāyashchitte … tirasi … ya as prajāghanee tanoo … swāhā idam vāyave …(2)

Om surya … yasai pashughnee … swāhā idam suryāya …(3)

Om Chadram yāsai greehaghnee…swāhā idam chandrāya …(4)

Om Gandharva … yasai yashoghnee …. Swāhā idam Gandharvāy …(5)

Again the groom connects with Brahmā and offers oblation with charu (oblation of rice, barley and pulse boiled for presentation to the gods and the Manes) into the Fire to the end of sacrificial remains of charu pot on reciting –

Om prajāpataye swāhā, idam prajāpatye

Again the groom performs 09 oblation with charu + ghee into prokshni pot reciting each Mantra for rectifying or Atonement as follows-

Om Bhooḥ Swāhā, idam bhooḥ …(1)

Om Bhuvaḥ Swāhā, idam bhuvaḥ …(2)

Om Swaḥ swāhā, idam Swaḥ …(3)

Om twanno Agne Varunarya vidwān devasya hedo Avayāsiseeshthā. Yajishtho Vahnitamaḥ shoshuchāno Viswā dweshān si pramumugdhyasmat Swāhā – idamangnee varunabhyām …(4)

Om sa twanno Agne Avamo Bhavotinedishtho Asyā ushaso vyushtho. Avayaksva no varunagvam Rarāno veeho Mudeekaṃ Suhavo Na odhi Swāhā idmagni varunā Bhyām …(5)

Im ayāshchāgne Asya Navi Shastipashcha

Satyamitvam Maya Asi. Ayāno gagyam Vahā syayano dhehi Bheshagagvam swāhā – idmaynaye …(6)

Om ye te shatam varuna ye sahasraṃ yagyiyā pasha vitatā Mahāntaḥ. Tebhirnno Adya savito at Vishnuh Vishwe Munchantu Marutaḥ Swarkkāh Swāhā, idam varināya savitre Vishnave Vishwebhyo Devebhyo Marudbhayaḥ Swarkkebhyaḥ …(7)

Om uduttamaṃ varuna pāshamasmad avādhamaṃ Vimadhyamagvam shrayāya. Athava yamādity a vrate tavānāgaso Aditaye syām swāhā, idam varunāya ...(8)

Om prajāpatye swāhā, idam prajāpatye ...(9)

Next rinse himself

Now donate remuneration to the Brahmā reciting –

Om asyām ratrou kreetaitat chaturthihom karmani

Kreeta-kreeta vekshanrup Brahma karma pratishthārtham purnapātram (256 fistful rice in potter bowl)

Prajāpati daivatam .... (spell name + clan) Brahmanāya

Brahmane dakshinaṃ tubhyamahaṃ Sampradade.

Next the groom sprinkles over his head out of preneeta pot water having paita reciting –

Om sumitrāyān Aapa oshadhayah santu.

Now turn down the Praneetā poṭ reciting –

Om durmitriyāh tasmai santu yosmān dweshti yancha vayaṃ dwishmah.

Next collect all spread kushas soaked with ghee be offered oblation into the Fire reciting –

Om deva Gātuvido Gātum Vittvagātumit Manasaspata

Iman deva yagyagvam swāhā, vātedhāh Swāhā.

Next the groom taking preethuda pot-water with mango leaves sprinkles over bride's head reciting –

Om yāte patighni prajaghni pashughnee Greehaghnee

Yashoghee ninditā tanoorgāraghnim tata enām karomi

Sā jiryatwam Mayā sah shree ... devi (spell name of the bride) – pray to ward off heinous nature of the bride.

Next the groom recites 04 Mantra and at the end of each Mantra

Om pranaiste prānām Sandadhāmi ...(1)

Om asthibhiste Astheeni sandodhāmi ...(2)

Om Māgvamsaiste māgvamsāni sandodhāni ...(3)

Om twachā te twachagvam sandadhāmi ...(4)

And the bride tastes the rest charu (porridge or hotchpotch).

Next the groom washes his hands and feet and touches the bride's heart resting through her shoulder to recite – Om yatte suseeme Hreedayan divi chandramasi shrigam. Vedāhaṃ tanmām tadvidyāt pashyem sharadah shatam geevem shatagvam shreenuyām saradaḥ shatam – wishing centenary life span.

Next taking fruit (Banana etc.) nut, flower and ghee and all be rested on the Sruva reciting in standing mode –

Om Moordhānam divo artim preethivyā vaiswānarmrit

Aajātmagnim kavigvam samrājmatithiem Janānām

Aasannā pātra Janyanta devāh swāhā.

Next the groom, while sitting, takes ashes of the burnt offering with ring finger of his right hand and touches his forehead uttering – trayāyusham jamadagne

Again touches with ashes his own neek uttering –

Om kashyapasya trayāyusham.

Again touches his own right arm root reciting –

Om yaddeveshu trayāyusham.

Again touches his heart reciting – Om tannostu trayāyusham

Now the groom donates precious coins or money as remuneration to the priest uttering –

Om Asyām Ratrou kreetaitad chaturthikarma pratishthārtham etavat (that money) dravyamulyaka

Hiranyamagni daivatam yathānāmgotrāy (spell name and clan of the priest) Brahmanāya Dikshinaham dade.

In the long run the groom donates profuse rememeration to ward off ill-omened happenings uttering –

Om Asyām rātrou kreetaitad savivah Chaturthi karmani nyoonādhika dosha parihārartham etāvat drovya (that money or precious stone placed or arranged)

Mulyaka Hirammagni Daivatam Nānānāmgotrevyo

Bhooyaseem Dakshinā dātumaham utsreeje – and tosses or cast off the coins among the spot-mates.

Chapter – 14

Quadrantal rite (chhandoga)

Now follow fire installation process as indicated in Chhandoga system earlier (12+21+6+6+6=51 fingers) and see the flaming straw blade in bronze dish uttering –

Om prajāpatih Rishih trishtupchhandah Agnih Devatā

Agnisthāpane viniyogaḥ.

Om kravyādimagnim prahinomi dooraṃ yamrājyam Gancchatu Ripravāhaḥ.

Next installs the Fire by placing the Fire-pot westward and the groom recites –

Prajāpatih Rishih Breehaticchandaḥ Breehaspatidevatā Agnisthapane viniyogaḥ.

Now the groom prays the Fire reciting Mantra –

Om ihaivāyamitaro Jātvedā Devebhyo havyam vahatu prajānaṇ.

Next the groom throws away Mango stalk (6"-7") soaked with ghee into the Fire silently.

Next the groom offers dress materials with flower, sandal paste, betel, waist lace, sacred thread and attire to the Brahma reciting –

Om Adya Matkartavya Chaturthi homkarmani kreetā-kreetā vekshanroop Brahmatwen ebhiḥ pushpa chandan Tāmbool yagyopaveet vāsobhih … gotram … sharmanam (speel name and clan of the Brahma) Brāhmanaṃ twāmahan Breene.

The Brahmā tells “Breetosmi” and the groom tells – “yathā vihitam karm kuroo” and the Brahmā responses as “Om Karvāni”.

Next the groom going around the northward sits on the south side.

Next the groom spreads tri-kush grass and stands westwardly and takes kush from Brahma’s seat with ring finger and thumb to throw away the kush grass to the S+W corner reciting –

Prajāpathi Rishih Agnirdevatā treenanirsane viniyogaḥ.

Om nirastaḥ parāvasuḥ.

Next the groom rinsing himself catches Brahma’s right hand and makes seated the Brahma to the south side of the Fire northwardly reciting –

Prajāpatih Rishih Aganirdevatā Brahmopveshane viniyogaḥ.

Om Aavasoḥ sadane seeda.

Next the groom placing tri-kush grass on Brahma’s head and recites –

Prajāpatih Rishih Gāyatricchandaḥ Vishnurdevatā jape viniyogaḥ. Om idaṃ vishnurvichakrame tredha nidadhe padam samoodhamasya pānsule.

The groom leaning down his right thigh and placing his right palm on his left palm downwardly to the earth and recites- parmeshthi Rishih Anushtupcchando Agnirdevatā Boomijape viniyogaḥ. Om idam bhumesbhajāmah idam Bhadraṃ sumangalaṃ. Parāspatnān Bādhaswāni eshān vindate Dhanaṃ.

Next the groom sweeps away the spot to the north side of the Fire uttering –

Koutsarishiḥ Jagateecchando Agnirdevatā preeshthasya shadhasya shashthe Ahani Agni Mārute shaste parisamoohane viniyogaḥ. Om imam stomam Arhate Jātvedase Rathmiva Sammahegā Manishayā. Bhadrāhi Naḥ pramatirasya sansadyagne sakhye Māri Shāmā Vayantava.

Again to the east side of the Fire-Altar recites –

Om bharomedhmaṃ krishnavāmā haveenshi te chinta-

Yat parvanā parvanā vayaṃ. Jeevātame pratarām

Sādhayā Dhiyogne sakhye Mārishāmā vayantav to the south side of the Fire Altar recites –

Om Shakam twā samidhaṃ sādhayā dhiyaste

Devā haviradantyāhutaṃ. Twamādityaṃ Aavahtām hyushmasyagne sakhye Mārishāmā Vayantava.

Now spread kushas around the Fire-Altar.

Next groom breaks 02 blades of kush reciting –

Prajāpatih Rishih pavitre devate pavitracchedane viniyogah.

Om pavitrestho Vaishnavyou.

Next the groom sprinkles holy water on the paita (02 blades) reciting –

Prajāpatih Rishih pavitredevate pavitrasammārjane Viniyogaḥ.

Om vishnormansā pootesthaḥ.

Next place paita in the ghee pot northwardly and pours ghee upon it and catching paita with ringfinger + thumb on resting his right fore arm upon his left arm to throw ghee-droops over his head reciting – prajāpatih Rishi Rajyam Devatā jyotpavane viniyogaḥ.

Om devastwā savitopunatu Achhidren pavitren vasoḥ Sooryasya Rashmibhiḥ.

Next sprinkle the paita with holy water and throws away into the Fire.

Next put up the ghee pot upon the Fire to be heated thrice.

Next the groom takes that ghee pot by his left hand and winnows the Sruva root with fore part of the kush on front side and sweeps away with the root part of the kush on the back side of the Sruva.

Now arrange water fall through hollowed palm reciting – prajāpatih Rishiḥ Aditidevatodakānjali prasechane viniyogaḥ. Om adite anumanyaswa.

Again arrange water-fall east faced with hollowed plam reciting –

Prajāpatih Rishih Anumatih Devatodakāngali prasecdhane viniyogaḥ. Om Anumate Anumanyaswa.

The groom having east-faced pours through hollowed palm to the north side of the Fire uttering –

Prajāpatih Rishiḥ saraswatee devatodkānjali prasechane viniyogaḥ. Om saraswatee Anumanyaswa.

Next arrange water-fall through hollowed plam around the Fire reciting –

Prajāpatih Rishiḥ trishtupcchandaḥ savitādevatā Agni-payukshane viniyogaḥ. Om devasavitah prasuvayagyam prasuva yagyapatiṃ Bhagāya Divyam Gandharvaḥ Ketapooḥ ketannaḥ punātu vachaspatiḥ Vāchannaḥ swadatu.

The groom sittig upon his feet takes one Mango stalk 6”-7” in his right hand upon his fisted lefthand reciting –

Parmeshthi Rishih Rudra Roopo … Brahmanah putrāya Namah as noted earlier.

Now ward off the kush grass to N+E corner offering flower + fruit to the Brahma leaning down his right thigh and the groom throws away one ghee-soaked stalk into the Fire.

Here offers oblation to the Fire reciting –

Prajāpatih Rishih Gāyatricchandaḥ Agnirdevatā vyāhriti-home viniyogaḥ, Om bhu swāhā …(1)

Pajāpalih Rishih ooshnikacchandoh vāyurdevata vyāhritihome viniyogaḥ; Om bhuwaḥ Swāhā ...(2)

Pajāpaliḥ Rishiḥ Anushtupcchandaḥ savitādevatā vyahritihome Viniyogaḥ. Om swaḥ swāhā. ...(3)

Pajāpatiḥ Rishiḥ Breehaticchando Breehaspatiḥ devatā Mahāvyahreetihome viniyogaḥ. Om Bhoobhuvaḥ swaḥ swāhā ...(4)

Again offering oblation to the Fire through the following Mantras (here the Rest of ghee drops be thrown into prokshanipot) projāpatih Rishih Agnirdevatā Chalurthee hom karmani viniyogaḥ; Om Agne prāyashchitte twaṃ devānāṃ prāyashchittirasi Brahmanastwā Nāttakām updhāvānmi Yāsyā pāpee Laxameeh tāmasyā Apajahi Swāhā ...(1)

Prajapatiḥ Rishih Vāyurdevatā chaturthihomkarmani viniyogaḥ. Om vāyoprāyashchitte twandevānām prāyshchittirasi Brahmanastwā Nāthkām upadhavāmi yāsyā patighwe tanoostāmasyā Apajahi Swāhā ...(2)

Prajāpatih ... Viniyogaḥ; Om chandre prāyashchitte ... swāhā ...(3)

Prajapatih ... Viniyogaḥ. Om surya ... swāhā ...(4)

Prajāpatih ... viniyogaḥ; Om Agnivāyuchandrasuryāh prāyashchitteyo gooyan devānām prāyashchittayaḥ stha Brāhmano vo nāthkām uadhavāmi yāsyā pāpeeh Laxmierya patighni yā Aputrayā yā Apashavyā Tanoostāmasyā Apajahat Swāhā. ...(5)

Next the groom sprinkles bride's head to toes. And the female folk make her bathed elsewhere.

Later on the groom speaks to the bride – "Kimatra pashyati"

And the bride responses – Bharttuh shree ... (name of the groom) Sharmno deerghāyushtwan.

Next both untie that knot of nativity and herbal bracelet and throws Mango stalk into the Fire silently.

Next both encircle the Fire with water & oblative materials reciting –

Prajapatiḥ Savitādevta Agniparyune viniyogaḥ;

Om devasavitaḥ prasuvayagyaṃ prasuva yagyapatiṃ Bhagāya divyo Gandharvaḥ ketapoo ketannaḥ punātu vachaspatih Vāchannaḥ swadatu.

Next repeat to arrange water fall as directed earlier.

Next bind spread kushas and soak with ghee thrice and throw away into the Fire uttering –

Prajāpatiḥ Rishiḥ Anushtupcchando Ruetrodratā darbhagootikā home viniyogaḥ; Om yaḥ pashoonāmadhipatee

Rudrastwan ticharo vreeshā pashoonasmākaṃ Mā hinseeretadastu hutam tava swāhā.

Now the groom and the bride touching their right hands performs concluding oblation with ghee, fruits, flower on the Sruva into the fire reciting –

Prajāpatih Rishih viradgāyatricchanda indrodevatā yashaskāmasya yaganeeya prayoge viniyogaḥ; Om ppornahomaṃ yashase juhomi yosmai Juhoti varamasmai dadāti varaṃ Breene yashasā Bhāmi loke swāhā.

Next the groom pours excess ghee into the fire reciting Om vasubhyaḥ swāhā.

Now repeat to appy ashes with ring finger to both hearts, right arms root, left arms root and foreheads reciting Mantra as directed above at suitable stanza.

Now the groom offers remuneration with filled rice potter pot to the Brahmā reciting –

Omadya kritaitat chaturthihom karmani kreeta-kreeta Vekshakāya Brahmane idam poornapātam prajapati daivatam … clan … sharmane (speel name and clan of the Brahmā) Brahmanāya dakshinamahaṃ dade (but in kush-made Brahma – changing for dakshinā namaḥ instead of Brahmanāy dekshinā-Mahan dade)

At last the groom performs ritual remuneration (Coins/money) to the priest (Ritual guide) taking sesame kush + holy water for renouncing that coins Money or precious stone on reciting-

Omadya kreetaitat Chaturthi Karma pratishthartham Cov-valved coins (speel the amount) gāmekām Rudra-daivatām (spell name and clan) gotrāya Brāhmanāya Dakshināmahaṃ Dade.

THE END

प्राच्य पाणिग्रहण प्रणाली की परम्परा के परिरक्षण एवं परिवर्धन हेतु सत्प्रयास की आवश्यकता है। वैश्विक पटल पर मानव-समाज की निरन्तर उभरती उत्कंठा के उत्क्रमण में प्राच्य पाणिग्रहण प्रणाली उपेक्षित हो रही है। इस परिस्थिति में वैदिक कर्मकाण्ड के उत्क्रमण एवं उद्घोष हेतु वैश्विक भाषान्तर विद्या की आवश्यकता है। अत: आशा है कि डॉ. मिश्र के द्वारा व्याख्यामूलक आड.ग्ल (अंग्रेजी) भाषान्तरण भावी पीढ़ी के लिए सार्थक सिद्ध होगा।

इति

By the patron